GUM

AND

THE MOTHER OF
MODERN CENSORSHIP

BY KAREN HARTMAN

★

★

DRAMATISTS
PLAY SERVICE
INC.

2

nent than that accorded the Author. The following acknowledgments must appear on the title page in all programs distributed in connection with performances of GUM:

Gum was originally developed in association with Page 73 Productions, Inc.

Gum was developed with support from The Playwrights' Center
Jerome Fellowship Program, Minneapolis, Minnesota.

Originally presented as a staged reading at Portland Stage Company
as part of the *Little Festival of the Unexpected*,
Christopher Akerlind and Anita Stewart, Artistic Directors,
Tom Werder, Managing Director.

Gum was originally produced by Center Stage, Baltimore, Maryland,
Irene Lewis, Artistic Director,
Peter W. Culman, Managing Director.

Originally produced in New York City in 1999 by
Women's Project and Productions,
Julia Miles, Artistic Director,
Patricia Taylor, Managing Director.

The following acknowledgment must appear on the title page in all programs distributed in connection with performances of THE MOTHER OF MODERN CENSORSHIP:

The Mother of Modern Censorship received its world premiere
at Circle X Theatre Company
(Jonathan Westerberg and Jim Anzide, Producing Artistic Directors)
in Los Angeles.

for Nicole

TABLE OF CONTENTS

ACKNOWLEDGMENTS 8

INTRODUCTION by Todd London 9

GUM 13

THE MOTHER OF MODERN CENSORSHIP
A Play in One Act 53

ACKNOWLEDGMENTS

These plays came into being through the accumulated inspiration and support of dozens of sources. Because this is my first acting edition, I wish to lay out the labyrinth of opportunities that have made it possible to keep writing for the theatre, but in the interests of space I offer the barest outline of those who have contributed directly to these two plays.

The Fulbright Foundation, the Jerome Foundation and grants from the Yale School of Drama supported their writing and development, and Douglas Jehl's sharp features for the *New York Times* inspired the subject matter. David Edgar and Maria Irene Fornes led workshops that sparked THE MOTHER OF MODERN CENSORSHIP and deepened my work on GUM, respectively. I am grateful for the creative companionship of Janet Allard and the other playwrights I studied with at Yale, both teachers and peers. Rachel Jacoby Rosenfield's friendship helped me view a year in Jerusalem through her uniquely acute analytical lens. Marjorie Allard insisted I apply for the Fulbright grant, then later became a savvy, patient guide in Cairo.

I owe deep thanks to some early collaborators on GUM whose work shaped my understanding of the play, particularly Jean Randich, Eleanor Holdridge, Laura Flanagan, Dale Soules, Kim D. Sherman and Anita Yavich. I am grateful to Tim Vasen, who championed GUM at Center Stage and directed the world premiere; to Kenn Watt and Kent Nicholson, who brought it to Larry Eilenberg's attention at the Magic Theatre; to Julia Miles and the staff of the Women's Project & Productions; and to Kathy Sova of Theatre Communications Group.

Although I was not a member of New Dramatists when I wrote these plays, it has become a cornerstone of my writing life.

In bringing about this DPS edition, my agent, Howard Rosenstone, has opened up a new future for these works.

INTRODUCTION

We are in a faraway country, a fictitious faraway country. Two girls, veiled head to toe, stand in a garden bounded by a high wall. They share a piece of gum.

This image — the opening moment of Karen Hartman's dazzling GUM — is a detail writ large, like the ones you find in art books, where a background scene played out in the shadow of a doorway is blown up for inspection. The walls loom, keeping the world out. The women's robes and veils — keeping their bodies under literal wraps — gain texture. In close-up, the girls' eyes become visible. They are shining with anticipation. This isn't a book of pictures, though; it's a play, blueprint for a living, breathing event, so we also hear the sound of giddy conspiracy, as one of the sisters says, "I have gum."

I dwell on this opening as a way of introducing Karen and her plays to you. It contains a concentrated dose of what I love about her work: its unexpectedness, the striking yet believable oddity of its setting, the charged vibrancy of its lyricism, its fusion of metaphor and reality, and, most important, the sheer physicality of its expression. Here gum is a tangible — chewable — fact. It is also a metaphor that spreads right through the bodies of the sisters who share it — a metaphor for pleasure, release, desire, transgression, America, the forbidden, the secret sexual act.

Look over these descriptions of gum, their juicy contraband: "Ordinary. And extraordinary. Hard at first, then sweet. I expected that break but there was none, only yielding. Easy to find a pulse. Everything went wet. And as I chewed I began to feel peculiar." Note how the actual and metaphorical infuse each other: "The juice of the gum became fire inside me." Hear how the words live in the body and express the body: "The spirit of the gum was conquering me. I moved in a new rhythm, as if my body chewed."

If GUM has the vivacity of a breakthrough play (and it does — you can feel the playwright's concerns and talents coming together in

9

a leap), THE MOTHER OF MODERN CENSORSHIP has the energy of the irrepressible, of a wild improvisation, a sly political goof. We are in another fictitious country (maybe it's the same one). Again there are two women onstage, middle-aged this time and presumably Middle Eastern, one in a long skirt, one in robes, headscarf and gloves. Each wears headphones plugged into a boom box on her desk. They listen to cassette tapes, stop the tapes, and throw them in the trash. They are the Chief Music Censor and her assistant. This easy mix of traditional and contemporary, East and West, is no less strange for its familiarity.

In GUM, the repression of sexual hunger, of the body — as if desire might be excised from the female body or desiring women severed from the body politic — takes a brutal, tragic turn. In THE MOTHER OF MODERN CENSORSHIP, repression takes a turn toward the absurd, as tape after tape goes in the can. The chief censor swears like a trucker. The novice censor sounds like Miss California ("I am very excited about a career in music censorship … I would like very much to be the conscience of society for a long time to come … "). And the women responsible for judging music and lyrics (even "deep breathing is a deep offense") have no access to or knowledge of the things they're hired to purge.

MOTHER, written first, was inspired by a *New York Times* article Karen brought to a workshop led by British playwright David Edgar at the Yale School of Drama in the mid-1990s. She had recently returned from a year of living in Jerusalem and traveling the Middle East, experiences that informed both the choice of the newspaper clipping and the play that emerged. Accompanying the article was a picture of three veiled women listening to Western pop music on headphones, searching for smut. Another article (also from Egypt) in the same paper nearly a year later, resulted in GUM. The story had a photo too: a pack of (allegedly aphrodisiac) gum with a picture of a (Spanish) fly on the box — "Splay" gum.

And so we are in faraway countries that fuse the fictitious and the real, the fabled and the factual. Time, though — and a publication date that nearly coincides with the first anniversary of the World

Trade Center and Pentagon attacks, and the subsequent war on Afghanistan's Taliban regime — has tilted them back toward their newspaper roots. When I read GUM now, I can't help thinking of stadium executions of women in Afghanistan and the fatal penalties imposed on rape victims (or of rape used as a tribal penalty) in Pakistan. The image of veiled women with headphones now seems less like a humorous invention than an ironic discovery. Plays that two years ago had an air of exoticism about them now feel almost journalistic. These examples of vibrant creative imagination have the added urgency of acts of cross-cultural empathy, conjured in a time of crisis. Fictitious or not, these countries are no longer faraway.

Karen Hartman's plays sing with life. Their remarkable vitality will be immediately apparent, as will the unique spirit and intelligence of the artist who bodied them forth. Like all great writing, they change and gain meaning over time. To read or see them is to watch them grow.

Todd London
November 2002
New York City

Todd London, Artistic Director of New Dramatists, is a winner of the George Jean Nathan Award for Dramatic Criticism and is author of The World's Room, *a novel.*

GUM

GUR

This play is dedicated to Maria Irene Fornes.

GUM began as a project for the Playwriting Program at the Yale School of Drama (Stan Wojewodski, Dean; Mark Bly, Chair of Playwriting), where it was produced as a workshop in New Haven, Connecticut, on January 23, 1997. It was directed by Eleanor Holdridge, with sets by Kris Stone, costumes by Anne Lalarb and Scott Pask, lights by Jane Shaw, sound by Malcolm Nicholls, dramaturgy by Scott Hamlin and stage management by Maureen Dunleavy. The cast was as follows:

RAHMI .... Sheryl Anderson
LINA .... Magaly Colimon
AUNTIE .... Annette Granucci
INAYAT .... Scott Reeves
YOUNG MAN .... Evan Dexter Parke

GUM was presented as a workshop production at the MACumba Festival by RJS Productions (now Page 73 Productions; Nicole Fix, Liz Jones, Asher Richelli and Daniel Shiffman, Producing Directors) in New York City on February 23, 1998. It was directed by Jean Randich, with original music by Kim D. Sherman, sets by Klara Zieglerova, costumes by Anita Yavich, lights by Matthew E. Adelson, sound by Robert Murphy and stage management by Joel Garland. The cast was as follows:

RAHMI .... Laura Flanagan
LINA .... Julia Dion
AUNTIE .... Dale Soules
INAYAT .... Michael Potts
YOUNG MAN .... Daniel Blinkoff

GUM premiered at Center Stage (Irene Lewis, Artistic Director; Peter W. Culman, Managing Director) in Baltimore, Maryland, on March 7, 1999. It was directed by Tim Vasen, with original music by Kim D. Sherman, sets by Myung Hee Cho, costumes by Anita Yavich, lights by Matthew Frey, sound by Sten Severson, dramaturgy by Jill Rachel Morris and stage management by Julianne Franz and Valerie Stedman Nolan. The cast was as follows:

RAHMI .... Miriam A. Laube
LINA .... Millie Chow
AUNTIE .... Dale Soules
INAYAT .... Joseph Kamal
YOUNG MAN .... Danyon Davis

GUM opened at the Magic Theatre (Larry Eilenberg, Artistic Director; Diane Terp, Managing Director) in San Francisco, California, on April 21, 1999. It was directed by Jean Randich, with original music by Kim D. Sherman, sets and lights by Rick Martin, costumes by Meg Neville, sound by David Molina and Chris Webb, dramaturgy by Kent Nicholson and stage management by Karen Runk. The cast was as follows:

RAHMI .... Laura Flanagan
LINA .... Esperanza Catubig
AUNTIE .... Helen Shumaker
INAYAT .... Aldo Billingslea
YOUNG MAN .... Omar Metwally

GUM opened at Women's Project & Productions (Julia Miles, Artistic Director; Patricia Taylor, Managing Director) in New York City on October 6, 1999. It was directed by Loretta Greco, with original music by Kim D. Sherman, sets by Myung Hee Cho, costumes by Elizabeth Hope Clancy, lights by Frances Aronson, sound by Obadiah Eaves, dramaturgy by Lisa McNulty and stage management by Renee Lutz. The cast was as follows:

RAHMI .... Daphne Rubin-Vega
LINA .... Angel Desai
AUNTIE .... Lizan Mitchell
INAYAT .... Firdous Bamji
YOUNG MAN .... Juan Rivera-Lebrón

CHARACTERS

RAHMI — a wealthy young woman, around twenty

LINA — Rahmi's sister, around eighteen

AUNTIE — Rahmi and Lina's late mother's sister, fifties

INAYAT — a merchant, mid- to late thirties

YOUNG MAN — same social class as the women, around twenty

DRESS

The women's clothing is modest, sumptuous and simple. Wealth can be expressed through fabric, jewelry and shoes. Rahmi wears an inheritence of heavy jewelry, including (possibly limited to) an elaborate gold bracelet. The sisters' dress is otherwise similar or identical. The men's clothing might be more Western.

SETTING

A walled garden adjoining a grand house in a fictitious faraway country. A bathing area is sometimes illuminated as part of the garden or within the house. The bath scenes create an illusion of privacy and distance from the rest of the home. Whenever possible, shifts in lighting will maintain momentum better than a physical change of scenery.

TIME

The present.

NOTE

GUM takes place in a fictional country and may be performed by actors of any race or ethnicity, in any combination.

GUM

One

The walled garden of a wealthy home. Rahmi waits, veiled from head to toe. Her sister Lina enters, equally covered. An air of conspiracy.

LINA. I have gum.
(They remove the headscarves.)
    Imported.
(They remove the face veils.)
    Juicy. Fruit.
(Lina unwraps the gum.)
RAHMI. No color.
LINA. Smell.
RAHMI. Ahh.
LINA. American.
RAHMI. Ohh.
LINA. You like to chew.
RAHMI. There is a ban.
LINA. Stop and swallow if they come.
RAHMI. They'll look inside me.
LINA. I will chew. *(Lina slips the gum into her mouth.)*
RAHMI. Gum is a secret. Burst of hidden flavor. I have not had the gray flat one.
LINA. Fruity.
RAHMI. I like the square bits of polished stone, each color so different but in your mouth the same. You slip the smoothness in and wait while sugar makes grit against your teeth. The first bite cracks the coating and your mouth goes sweet and liquid all at once. You can hold it down and suck. You can mold it around each tooth and up into the pink of your mouth. Most I like to chew.

21

LINA. Juicy.

RAHMI. Still?

LINA. American. High quality.

RAHMI. I will go mad.

LINA. Share mine. *(Lina takes the wad of gum out of her mouth and splits it. They chew.)*

RAHMI. I like it.

LINA. What happened that day?

RAHMI. At first I thought the feeling came because I was alone with men in the car. But gradually I started to wish one of them was with me in the back seat. I was so easy. I found no resistance. You know the rest.

LINA. Where did you buy that gum?

RAHMI. They offered it.

LINA. How did you meet those men?

RAHMI. We know them from school.

LINA. What did it feel like?

RAHMI. Ordinary. And extraordinary. Hard at first, then sweet. I expected that break but there was none, only yielding. Easy to find a pulse. Everything went wet. And as I chewed I began to feel peculiar.

LINA. Where?

RAHMI. You know where.

LINA. What did they do?

RAHMI. My memory goes.

LINA. Have more. *(Lina gives Rahmi the rest of her gum.)*

RAHMI. A boy's finger brushed my lips and under the veil to the skin of my neck. Another boy removed my shoe.

LINA. Merciful God protect each step you take.

RAHMI. The juice of the gum became fire inside me. There was heat each place they touched, and the special place.

LINA. What place?

RAHMI. The spirit of the gum was conquering me. I moved in a new rhythm, as if my body chewed. I bit the first boy's hand. I took his wrist in my mouth and licked and gnawed like a bone. I curled my foot through the other boy's hair.

LINA. Praise God who keeps you clean.

RAHMI. Out the window I saw upside-down sky. We were

noplace. It was day. I wanted to be exposed. I let them unwrap me like a package. They lifted my body and spread the dress. Fear rose. I swallowed it. The gum moved from my belly down. Hands touched inside my legs.

LINA. Loving God.

RAHMI. It was just. like. gum! But more difficult. And better.

INAYAT. *(Offstage.)* Fragrant blossom!

LINA. A strange man is in our home. *(The girls hurry to replace the veils.)*

RAHMI. You said nothing.

LINA. You were chewing.

RAHMI. Bring more gum.

LINA. It costs.

RAHMI. I shared.

LINA. Swallow. *(They swallow. They are covered. Inayat enters, a middle-class man, late thirties.)*

INAYAT. Two modest girls. Delightful. Which is Rahmi? I come bearing gifts. Show me Rahmi. *(The girls hold still.)* You have permission to reveal your face. *(The girls hold still.)* Delightful. *(Inayat closes his eyes and sniffs. He walks to Lina.)* You are the second sister.

LINA. Lina.

INAYAT. Accept a token, Lina. *(He places a small perfume vial in Lina's hand and sniffs his way to Rahmi.)* And here is Rahmi.

RAHMI. Am I a shrub? Are you a dog? Stop sniffing.

INAYAT. Rahmi. I think about women all the time, but I want you. I love your anger. I love your complicated scent. And in our window of closeness I felt myself belonging and exploring. A flash of what seemed impossible. This flash will become a fire. The fire a hot room. And in this room I will lay you down and worship you the rest of my days. *(Silence.)*

RAHMI. Have we met?

INAYAT. Look through the crack in your garment. It is Inayat. I sold you that perfume.

RAHMI. A merchant?

INAYAT. Think back.

RAHMI. Lina, call Father. Call Auntie.

INAYAT. Your guardians are watching from the house.

RAHMI. They will see you smelling us and be angry.

23

INAYAT. Could you love me? *(Silence.)*
LINA.

True love is like a seed
Planted and nurtured by a wise hand.
True love is not a weed
Growing wild and wasteful where it may land.

(Silence.)
INAYAT. Remove the veil, Rahmi. You're mine.
LINA. I will fetch tea. *(Lina exits. Silence.)*
INAYAT. Cigarette?
RAHMI. *(Lowering the veil.)* Yes.
INAYAT. It is a scandalous habit. *(She smokes.)*
RAHMI. What's the worst thing you ever did?
INAYAT. Tortured a monkey. I was young.
RAHMI. Did you burn it?
INAYAT. We pulled it apart.
RAHMI. How brutal.
INAYAT. It was a beast. You are a girl, smooth from brow to toe.
RAHMI. I could wax you a monkey.
INAYAT. Then we would each have a secret.
RAHMI. A monkey might be easier to tame.
INAYAT. I sold you the scent and you met my eye. A wealthy girl, unchaperoned. You left and I blended that look. *(He produces a beautiful perfume vial.)* Black-eyed Lady of the Veil. Lovely. Crazy. Inside sweet and clear. This fragrance is making me rich. I had to find the girl. May I?
RAHMI. Yes. *(He bends to apply the perfume.)*
INAYAT. I smell something else.
RAHMI. Could you get me gum? *(Lina enters with tea.)*
LINA. Auntie says not to smoke in front of men. The parting of the lips, the intensified breathing, the deliberate insertion, removal, and reinsertion of an object into a young girl's mouth all are very suggestive. Tea? *(Rahmi puts out her cigarette. All take tea.)*
INAYAT. So many of God's fine gifts appeal to more than one orifice. There is the pleasing sight of your family's quality tea service. The enticing clink of cups on the tray. An aroma of fine leaves. Wet steam inside one's mouth. And of course, the taste.
LINA. Tea is permitted.

24

INAYAT. But even tea is dark, sweet, and hot as the heart.

RAHMI. More please.

INAYAT. Would that satiate you?

LINA. We like tea.

INAYAT. But you want gum.

RAHMI. Yes.

INAYAT. Gum is not for virgins anymore.

RAHMI. Oh.

INAYAT. Certain nations envy our women, the purest and most erotic in the world. They seek to undo you, so they tamper with your gum. Young ladies bite, chew, and lose their ground. Alarming stories have spread. Officials toil to isolate the bad gum by locating a foreign ingredient. The current theory is: this gum accentuates a woman's own ... element. Identification is tricky. Thus the ban.

LINA. *(Politely.)* Oh my.

INAYAT. Perhaps in your nice garden or experimenting at university you have missed the news.

LINA. We forget to pay attention.

RAHMI. What does my father think?

INAYAT. Your father seems eager. The contract remains to be settled. But I think he is flexible.

RAHMI. My father? Flexible? Something is wrong.

LINA. Inayat mixed perfume for old Auntie.

INAYAT. Clean-billed Parrot of the South.

LINA. Colorful yet immaculate. Won't she like that? People treat Auntie like she's already gone, but she wants to be noticed like everyone else.

RAHMI. I will go mad.

LINA. She's having a pain.

INAYAT. Doctors can look.

LINA. No thank you.

RAHMI. I will die.

INAYAT. Does this happen?

LINA. Rahmi is fragile.

INAYAT. That's fine.

LINA. Rahmi. We can shop for wedding cloth, you and me. We can feel every kind until you choose the best one. We can find special shoes.

INAYAT. What a nice treat. Shop with your sister, my Rahmi. Once we are married you will see her less and less. I will learn my way around your body. We will each become the other's whole world.

RAHMI. I will shop.

INAYAT. Delightful.

RAHMI. For a short dress. *(Lina and Inayat laugh.)*

INAYAT. Oh my.

RAHMI. For platters of olives and gum.

INAYAT. She will be an adventure.

RAHMI. For a ticket away.

LINA. No!

INAYAT. Lina, you had a package from America.

LINA. Language cassettes for school. I am grateful. *(Lina exits.)*

INAYAT. Be as difficult as you wish.

RAHMI. I want it. Imported and wrapped.

INAYAT. Will you marry me?

RAHMI. It seems I will.

INAYAT. Whom do you love?

RAHMI. I love Lina. And pleasure.

INAYAT. Gum is your way.

RAHMI. Yes.

INAYAT. Like a wild-eyed bird you will nest.

Two

Night. Rahmi kneels in prayer.

RAHMI. May that feeling return.
(Rahmi slowly arcs back.)

Three

Morning. Lina is listening to a walkman, unveiled. She lies back and begins to unwrap herself, experimenting.

LINA. Like a package. *(Rahmi enters, unveiled.)*
RAHMI. I was flatter than that. In a car. And not alone. *(Lina turns away.)*
  What music did she send you? Are there photographs? Does she wear jeans now? It's why I study science. Scientists go everywhere. Women work in labs with only protective glasses.
  I bet I could understand that song. Give it.
  There are two kinds of people. The ones who go free and the ones who sit and smell till they die.
  Give it or I'm going away. *(Lina gives Rahmi the walkman. Rahmi listens.)*
  Where's the music? Our cousin in America sends you actual lessons? Words words words. You are such a little pigeon.
LINA. Father says you're lucky and to act it.
RAHMI. Pigeon.

Four

Night. Rahmi is reading a biology book (no language visible). Lina is reading an American novel. No veils. Their words here are unspoken thoughts, inaudible to one another.

RAHMI. *(Reading.)* A group of cells is like a group of men. They live collaboratively for the community. When a cell senses it is no longer of use to its larger organism, it kills itself. Programmed cell death, or apoptosis, is characteristic of healthy bodies. In this way

each organism stays clean and alive.
(Imagining.)
>I am a fish swimming in tea.
>Bird flying over the fire.
>Turtle crawling out of the pot.
>With no sister at all.

(Back to text.)
Cells attach to a basement membrane, or ground, which tells them what to do. The ground determines a cell's function and size. If a cell breaks from the ground, it receives no instruction and may die or mutate. The free-floating cell may grow without stopping, invading the basement membrane and displacing normal activity.
(Imagining.)
>I break from ground.
>I grow without stopping.
>I float free!

(Back to text.)
This is cancer. It cannot be reversed and is controlled by excision.

LINA. She has been wild like a creature since we were small.

>And they said learn your own ways Lina.
>Think of her as the wrong example.
>Learn your own ways.
>But to me you have always been the strongest and most beautiful girl. I wish I could make you happy.
>I wish I was you.
>To me you have been the biggest sister.

(They go back to reading a while. Rahmi puts down her book and sings a familiar song out loud. Lina listens.)

RAHMI. *(Sings.)*
>Aiiii aiii aiii
>Bird fly so high
>She find the sky and go down
>Down to ground.
>
>Why aiii aiii
>She cry aiii aiii
>They let her die and go down
>Down to ground.

LINA and RAHMI. *(Together sing:)*
    The world is wide
    And I walk across
    And my father's fields never end.
    The rain is sweet
    And the wind is warm
    And my life is an easy day.
LINA. *(Continues alone, a rare verse.)*
    Eeee eeee eeee
    She come to me
    And blood flow free falling down
    Down to ground.

    I aiii aiiii
    Lie aiii aiii
    Wrapped in leaf of green
    I am clean.
(Rahmi looks at Lina.)

Five

Lina and Inayat drink tea.

INAYAT. Five o'clock?
LINA. That's what she said, sir.
INAYAT. Call me brother.
LINA. Let us wait to be informal.
INAYAT. You were raised well.
LINA. Rahmi and I the same.
INAYAT. You protect each other.
LINA. Yes.
INAYAT. You would not give me information.
LINA. No.
INAYAT. Not for anything I have.

29

LINA. We are a wealthy family, as you know.

INAYAT. Does she love me?

LINA. My sister is capable of great passion.

INAYAT. She is a religious woman?

LINA. She prays.

INAYAT. Why would she be late?

LINA. Father gives the driver too much to do.

INAYAT. I won't be able to hire men and cars.

LINA. She knows.

INAYAT. Does she cook?

LINA. The bride price was given, yes?

INAYAT. I heard a story concerning your sister.

LINA. You smell so good.

INAYAT. Oh.

LINA. Do you create a special cologne or is it just the atmosphere?

INAYAT. Certain notes of citrus, musk, and spice blend to heighten one person's awareness of another.

LINA. What can I get you?

INAYAT. Did she ravage two boys in a car?

LINA. No.

INAYAT. Have you ever loved so much you would believe anything?

LINA. I am very young.

INAYAT. So you are.

LINA. And love grows, once arranged.

INAYAT. Still.

LINA. She'd pretend she was a northern spy who had replaced my real sister. "Rahmi is dead," she would say. "Tell me her secrets." I'd scream, "They will die with my sister." We would play Torture.

INAYAT. You succumbed?

LINA. Never.

INAYAT. What next?

LINA. Rahmi would outwit the spy and reappear. She'd kiss me for being true.

INAYAT. In your opinion this violent impulse is gone.

LINA. Absolutely.

INAYAT. Why does she threaten to leave? *(Rahmi enters.)*

RAHMI. Borders borders BORDERS.

INAYAT. Did you ravage two men in a car?

RAHMI. No.

INAYAT. Praise God who keeps us clean.

RAHMI. I've seen cells before but looking through the scope today I knew. Inside our body are more bodies, establishing separate identities, making membranes. Dividing and dividing so each little cell has his own skin. I'm sick of it.

INAYAT. Such divisions make us human.

RAHMI. Why can't we be one whole thing?

INAYAT. That is a marriage.

RAHMI. Separate people. I'm sick of it. Countries. Rules. Membrane. I'm sick sick SICK of it. We take a cat and split it into organs. We slice the organs and make samples. In the samples we find more and more teeny separate parts.

INAYAT. If we were one whole thing you couldn't experiment. What would you cut and examine?

RAHMI. Why cut?

LINA. I should study.

RAHMI. Who made knives?

INAYAT. Sometimes we need things in more manageable bits. We remove what is poisonous, unwanted, or unclean.

RAHMI. No.

INAYAT. I have gum. Imported. Would you like a piece, Lina?

LINA. Yes please.

INAYAT. It's wrapped. What an upsetting boundary. *(Inayat stares at Rahmi as he unwraps the gum. A sexual act in miniature. He hands it to Lina.)* Good girl. *(Lina breaks it with her teeth and gives half to Rahmi. They chew.)* Your attachment to gum is reckless, girlish and sweet. Upon marriage I will teach you grown-up pleasure. *(Inayat unwraps a piece of gum, chews.)* Confirm one thing for me. It's about your body. *(Lina deliberately spills tea on Rahmi.)*

RAHMI. OWW.

LINA. Oh.

RAHMI. Stupid frog.

LINA. Oh no. Your whole lap. Poor thing.

RAHMI. HOT!

LINA. Let me peel off your —

INAYAT. *(Rising to leave.)* I must —

LINA. She was practically on time, you see?

INAYAT. Peace over you.

RAHMI. OWW!

LINA. Peace. *(Inayat exits.)*

RAHMI. That hurt. *(Lina slaps Rahmi.)*

LINA. Yes it hurts.

RAHMI. Ow.

LINA. How did we grow up in the same house?

RAHMI. I'm going.

LINA. They will find you and cut you and change you. *(Silence. Lina unwraps Rahmi's skirt and puts cold water on the burn. More silence. Rahmi watches Lina.)*

RAHMI. I remember when you started hiding under the bath water.

LINA. Some places don't get clean.

RAHMI. Did you get Clean? *(Pause.)*

LINA. Yes.

RAHMI. You never said.

LINA. Auntie took me on Holiday. *(Pause.)*

RAHMI. You were so small.

LINA. Yes.

RAHMI. How can a child hide pain?

LINA. It's possible.

RAHMI. Why not me?

LINA. Maybe you were an experiment.

RAHMI. I failed.

LINA. No. No. *(Lina kneels at Rahmi's feet, arms around her legs.)*

Six

Night. In the garden Lina listens to the walkman, veiled. Rahmi is in the bath. Auntie sits beside her, fully dressed. There is a sense of privacy and distance between the two simultaneous scenes.

AUNTIE. The best thing you can do for your body is hide the smell.

I wish she'd left boys. Boys you must keep from their own cruel ways, but girls — praise God who makes us as He will — girls try me. I want to hold each one like a secret chocolate, sweet and dissolving in the first hot wind.

I brought your fine jasmine soap. Wash good.

We are not honest people. It hurts me watching girls grow up to see. You chase what you shouldn't. You shed me like skin.

Let the water in deep, Rahmi dear. It's clean.

Yes, God split hot desire into ten parts and gave us nine.

I have been a widow for a very long time.

LINA. *(Repeating a tape in English.)* Use the meter, please. *(Pause.)* Use the meter, please. *(Pause.)* Use the meter or I'll take down your number and report you. *(Pause.)* I'm not a stupid immigrant.

AUNTIE. I want you washing. Not just sit there and soak. I bought a new loofah and a brush for your nails and a clipper for dead skin and tweezers.

LINA. Hands to yourself.

AUNTIE. When were you last waxed? I saw hair.

LINA. *(Overlapping on "saw.")* I don't need help.

AUNTIE. What about your period? *(Pause.)* Your mother and I go to the doctor one time and she bleeds all over his face. We laugh and laugh, he gets more puffed-up and more quiet. Then all at once he yells, "I AM LOST IN THE FLOOD!" Little drops from his eyeglasses, a streak on his nose, bloody hair. We laugh and laugh. We were only girls. We worried there was something wrong. That's why we were there. Two years she wasn't bleeding.

(Starts to laugh.) We walk in so scared. "She's not bleeding," I say. Both of us so pale. She wants me with her. I'm grown. "She's not bleeding," I say and they strip her down and tip her over and look inside and WHOOSH. Like a river. Like a joke we made together.

LINA. Get the fuck away from me. *(Pause.)* FIRE! *(Her own thought.)* Why fire? *(Lina rewinds the tape.)*

AUNTIE. This doctor is a lady. She just wants to check. *(Inayat sneaks into the garden and watches Lina from behind.)*

INAYAT. Rahmi.

33

RAHMI. *(To Auntie.)* I'm washing. *(Inayat creeps up behind Lina.)*

LINA. *(Softly.)* Use the meter, please. Use the meter or —

AUNTIE. I want to see steam.

LINA. *(Continuous with tape.)* I'll take down your number and report you.

RAHMI. *(Continuous with Auntie.)* Lina burned me.

LINA. I'm not a stupid immigrant.

AUNTIE. That was clumsy.

LINA. Hands to yourself.

RAHMI. It hurts!

LINA. I don't need help.

AUNTIE. Life hurts.

LINA. Get the fuck away from me. FIRE! *(Inayat touches Lina from behind. The walkman falls to the ground.)*

INAYAT. Rahmi, I have wanted you hard. *(Lina turns and kisses him on the mouth. He sees her face.)* Sweet Lina?

LINA. When you marry my sister you must touch her this way again and again.

INAYAT. It's Lina.

LINA. Promise? Promise?

INAYAT. Yes. *(Inayat runs away, crashing loudly.)*

AUNTIE. *(Calling to the garden.)* LINA DEAR!

LINA. *(From the garden, an explanation.)* I FELL!

RAHMI. She is so careless suddenly.

AUNTIE. Take advantage of your softened skin to scrape some off. Brush and pluck and clip.

(Lina picks up the walkman and sees it has broken.)

Seven

The garden. Day. Lina enters carrying a package. She sings her own American love song.

34

LINA.
Oh moon, doo woo woo
You left me standing, doo woo woo
Oh moon, doo woo woo
Understanding, doo woo woo
Handing me, doo woo woo woo
The key, doo woo woo woo
Doo woo woo you.
Doo woo woo true.
(She opens the package.)
Oh sun, doo woo woo
My heart is breaking, doo woo woo
No fun, doo woo woo
My body aching.
Taking sides,
Making brides, doo woo woo woo
Doo woo woo she.
Doo woo woo me.
Doo woo woo plea?
(Lina removes several cassettes from the package and opens them. Instead of tapes, piles of gum fall out of the cases. She unwraps many pieces, shoves them in her mouth, and chews. Rahmi enters holding aloft a package from a fancy shop.)
RAHMI. I passed!
LINA. *(Mouth full.)* Have gum.
RAHMI. Celebration!
LINA. *(Cold.)* Now you can marry.
RAHMI. I want music.
LINA. It broke.
RAHMI. What is wrong with you?
LINA. How did you pass?
RAHMI. I said we've spent a lot of time on horses.
LINA. That's true.
RAHMI. We should study.
LINA. Do you love him best?
RAHMI. No one wants me around anymore.
LINA. *(Disagreeing.)* No …
RAHMI. People look at you like a bright thing they didn't expect

to find. I'm just a difficult girl.

LINA. What happened to Mother's bracelet?

RAHMI. *(Proud.)* I gave it to the doctor. First I told her what they would do if I failed. Then I gave the bracelet. She had on American shoes. I think I'll be a doctor.

LINA. You will get caught.

RAHMI. You'll get caught. You smuggle gum.

LINA. You wanted it.

RAHMI. You were going to chew it all yourself.

LINA. No.

RAHMI. You should want more.

LINA. I want.

RAHMI. What's the worst thing you ever did?

LINA. Lied.

RAHMI. When?

LINA. You know when. *(Glancing at Rahmi's package.)* Is that your wedding cloth?

RAHMI. Auntie took me right to the shop. When?

LINA. I could tell you weren't a spy.

RAHMI. So?

LINA. For example.

RAHMI. Do you know what almost happened to me?

LINA. Twelve years I didn't tell you what happened to me and now it's like nothing. You are selfish. I am going to chew and chew. *(Lina exits. Rahmi wraps herself in the cloth. A young man appears at the top of the garden wall.)*

YOUNG MAN. *(Sings.)*
    Give me
    A give me
    A give me your loving
    Your sweet body
    Give me
    A give me
    A give me more.
(He waits.)
    Want me
    A want me
    A want me closer
    So so closer

36

Want me
I know you
I know how you do.
(Spoken.) I know how you do.

RAHMI. That's my father's wall.

YOUNG MAN. You sing.

RAHMI. *(Sings.)*
When it is spring I will hear you
Like my voice
My own voice
Inside.

YOUNG MAN. Come out of there. Let's play.

RAHMI. Why didn't you come sooner?

YOUNG MAN. I have gum.

RAHMI. Yes?

YOUNG MAN. You will feel just like before. *(Rahmi climbs onto the wall. Lina is revealed in the bath.)* Someone will see.

RAHMI. Father is away. Auntie is asleep. Lina is in the bath.

YOUNG MAN. I don't like danger.

RAHMI. Give me that gum.

YOUNG MAN. Some people do. But you, me, and Omar, we like pleasure.

RAHMI. I'm sick of being a girl.

YOUNG MAN. If you were a boy then you, me, and Omar would have to find a girl.

RAHMI. I want that gum.

YOUNG MAN. Come closer.

RAHMI. No one understands me. No one understands my body. Since then.

YOUNG MAN. The gum is in the car. So is Omar.

RAHMI. Tell the truth.

YOUNG MAN. We want to do it again. Don't you?

RAHMI. Yes.

YOUNG MAN. Okay.

RAHMI. They could stone me to death on this wall.

YOUNG MAN. Probably not.

RAHMI. They choose stones of a particular size. No pebbles — too cruel. No boulders — too mercifully quick. Each man takes a rock and they crush you part by part. Jaw. Breast. Eye. Until the last stone snaps your neck.

YOUNG MAN. Nothing will happen.

RAHMI. *(Climbing down.)* I'm different now. Full of honor. See that cloth?

YOUNG MAN. Me and Omar like the noise you make. *(Rahmi hurls a stone at the young man and hits his eye. He jumps down and away, crashing loudly.)*

LINA. *(In the bath.)* RAHMI!

RAHMI. I fell!

AUNTIE. *(Off, from somewhere within the house.)* Clumsy. *(Rahmi enters the bathing area, goes to Lina and stands by the tub.)*

RAHMI. I apologize.

LINA. People are waiting to do things to you. That's how it is.

RAHMI. No.

LINA. People say spy when they mean sister. People say holiday when they mean a scary thing.

RAHMI. I promise we won't ever be like that anymore.

LINA. People say me when they mean you.

RAHMI. Lina. I'm sorry I let you hide all that time.

LINA. Oh. *(Rahmi takes off her dress.)*

RAHMI. Can I wash you?

LINA. Yes. *(Rahmi steps into the tub. A moment of quiet. Auntie appears.)*

AUNTIE. Like when you were small and I would wash first one and then the other. You so still, you bigger and squirming almost out of the tub. Until I let you both go and said, you do. You do. The child who drowns in a bathtub is stupid. I was right outside the door. You're ladies now, but I am right outside the door. *(Pause.)* I have more soap if you need. *(Auntie exits. Rahmi washes Lina. Slow. The sisters breathe together.)*

LINA. Can I ask a question? *(Pause.)*

     What is It? *(Pause. Rahmi takes Lina's hand down into the water.)*

     Here?

RAHMI. *(Pleasure.)* Yes.

LINA. *(A different pleasure.)* Yes.

Eight

Auntie and Inayat drink tea. She is working with the wedding cloth.

INAYAT. They said four o'clock?

AUNTIE. Lina is very reliable. Rahmi too of course, reliable.

INAYAT. I want to be faithful to my wife, and the unfortunate truth is we abuse what we own. Rahmi cannot be owned. I will treat her like precious glass.

AUNTIE. More men should think like you. I always felt like old tin. Battered.

INAYAT. I want her wild like hair that you wrap in a scarf.

AUNTIE. You paid a large price.

INAYAT. If I set my pigeon free, I want to know it's coming back. That is the pleasure of letting go: knowing that you are not, in fact, ever losing anything at all.

AUNTIE. Can you fix things?

INAYAT. Yes of course. *(She holds out Lina's walkman.)*

AUNTIE. Lina broke this somehow.

INAYAT. *(Recognizing it.)* Oh. *(Pause.)* It's not so bad, see? This bit here won't shut, that's all. Needs to be wedged back … the spring. There.

AUNTIE. Thank you.

INAYAT. Everything's mendable.

AUNTIE. Good.

INAYAT. The contract mentions British crystal. Does it have to be —

AUNTIE. British crystal.

INAYAT. I hire fine glassblowers for the shop.

AUNTIE. It was her last chance to make a demand. You signed it.

INAYAT. In exchange for my adult virgin bride.

AUNTIE. Smell.

INAYAT. Clean-billed Parrot of the South.

AUNTIE. You have transformed me. First thing every morning I

breathe a mix of warmth and fragrance and it is myself. I've gone
vain like a young girl stretching before a mirror.

INAYAT. It hasn't been so long for you.

AUNTIE. We had no mirrors in my home. If a woman looks too
closely at herself, she'll fall in love. And lovers are useless.

INAYAT. You must have been a romantic person once.

AUNTIE. There were no movies growing up. Now girls see all
kinds of things.

INAYAT. That's changing back.

AUNTIE. I remember when suddenly there were no veils in the city.

INAYAT. I was a young man.

AUNTIE. It was obscene.

INAYAT. Different hairs on women's heads. Curly and straight,
poorly maintained, parted. Right in public.

AUNTIE. Better now.

INAYAT. If I want a Western girl I can rent one.

AUNTIE. Precisely.

INAYAT. I won't, anymore.

AUNTIE. Rahmi is particularly passionate, you know. Never cir-
cumcised.

INAYAT. Her doctor explained that the organ itself does not nec-
essarily cause promiscuity.

AUNTIE. They say it's better for the man.

INAYAT. I prefer uncircumcised prostitutes.

AUNTIE. Yes?

INAYAT. There are more possibilities. And they seem to enjoy it,
even the very poor girls who have no choice.

AUNTIE. How can you tell?

INAYAT. The way they move. Certain sounds. More frequent
orgasms.

AUNTIE. I should think.

INAYAT. In a wife though, it is a risk.

AUNTIE. A wild thing.

INAYAT. She passed the exam. And if I should ever see reason to
be concerned, I will order the operation.

AUNTIE. I made that very clear to Rahmi.

INAYAT. You love her like a mother.

AUNTIE. My sister had female complications her whole life.

Things ripped and restitched. She wept when Rahmi was born, made me promise never to cut her girl. I told my sister Lina was a boy. She was dying and I said, "Kiss your son." Life is a big sack of lies.

INAYAT. But to a purpose. Lina is well-behaved. And Rahmi is marrying me. *(A burst of girlish laughter offstage. Lina leads Rahmi in by the hand. They are ebullient.)*

LINA. Hello! *(Kisses Auntie.)* Auntie, you smell so nice. We brought you a gift. *(Beautiful cloth.)* You belong in fine things. We took a long time to choose.

AUNTIE. Never mind. What a texture. This is for a much younger woman.

RAHMI. I'm getting married. Everyone should rejoice.

INAYAT. Your Auntie will be the lady of the house.

AUNTIE. Not I. Lina.

RAHMI. We will share Lina. She'll stay with me sometimes. And one day you'll live with me, too. It's a fine contract. Nothing changes. When this is my house we will all be here again.

INAYAT. If you choose.

RAHMI. I will choose.

INAYAT. By then I may have built you a perfume palace so grand that you forget all other bonds. *(He gives her gum.)*

RAHMI. Yum.

AUNTIE. Mr. Inayat!

INAYAT. Authorities know this is a respectable home. We can do as we like. I am accountable for her pleasure, however greedy she gets.

RAHMI. Mmm.

INAYAT. Chew and chew.

RAHMI. Mmm.

INAYAT. Lina?

LINA. Oh no thank you.

AUNTIE. *(Of wedding cloth.)* Look at this stitching.

LINA. So fine.

AUNTIE. Are the sleeves right?

LINA. Oh yes. Very roomy.

AUNTIE. You try.

LINA. I can't fit it over the veil.

INAYAT. I'm family.

41

AUNTIE. Hold it up, then. *(Lina holds up the dress.)*
RAHMI. Beautiful you.
AUNTIE. One day.
LINA. I'm just ordinary.
AUNTIE. Everyone finds love.
LINA. Rahmi first.
RAHMI. Look at you.
LINA and RAHMI. Don't get married. *(Everyone laughs. The young man climbs onto the wall. His eye is bandaged.)*
YOUNG MAN.

>Hello.
>We say you want a ride
>and she say what's that
>and I say a ride is where you get in the car and we drive you to where no one sees and we touch you till you're slidey and groaning and we bite you and grab fists of your hair and your robe creeps up and you squirm and twitch closer and wider and he watch and touch and I put all I got inside you
>till you start to move and when you're going I go with you and everything we have is locked and rubbing and he's a-watchin and a-strokin your hair and he's saying baby you look so good to me like that, baby you're makin me want you too, open wider lift your hips so I can see, and you do everything he say and you love it more and more and you make me crazy the way you push and I give it up for you
>uh huh
>but you yell touch me hard, and push my hand against you and your face go red and you lose your breath and me and him go yeah baby uh huh baby that's right, me holding your thighs him eating your neck and you relax
>and he go you make me hot
>and you go more, I can take more
>and I slide my hands up your legs and up your back and pull your robe till it cover your face and we touch and touch you, four hands all over your body feel so mysterious and I lift the cloth over your head and you look down at your flesh with hands on it and a mouth at your breast and cupping your belly and sweaty and slimy and I whisper you are so beautiful, turn over baby

and you do
but I stay in front flicking my tongue on your face while he
stroke and
spread and
enter you
a little harder than you want, a little faster
I say you're doin so good baby that's right
and you're jerkin back on him now, rough, and your face
start to change and I push fingers in your mouth and you bite and
I slide my hand out your mouth and down your neck and between
your breasts and down and down to pulse one finger
right there
while he push and rest, push and rest and you start to scream
and I say baby I like the noise you make and he moan and you
scream and both of you go tense and wet together and he grab
your breasts and pull you way against him so deep you scream
again
and collapse
both of you
on me.
That's a ride, baby.
And she bite her gum and go,
okay.
(Everyone looks at Rahmi. She is smiling. Blackout. A terrible high-pitched sound.)

Nine

Lina finishes building a house of gum wrappers.

LINA. *(Sings.)*
I will weep in my sleep for you.
I will cry till I die
till the blood run out my eye

till the sigh and the why and the try
make a braid and lie flat.
I lie flat.

I will scream in my dream for you.
I will fold till I'm cold
till my paper house is sold
till I'm old till I'm bold till I'm rolled
like a wrapper and flat.
I lie flat.

I will make a new place for you.
For two.
I'll be true.

(Rahmi enters, followed by Auntie. Rahmi walks with a cane.)

AUNTIE. I thought we could use a treat. Mmm. Sweets before breakfast. I got your favorite, and yours. Mmm. And mine. Did you know his shop was open so early? Quiet outside. No traffic. I've been such a lazy woman my whole life. I might stop sleeping late now. I might like a row of mornings just like this.

RAHMI. Since when did you collect those?

LINA. A long time.

RAHMI. Why?

LINA. Do you like it?

RAHMI. It's great. That must have taken forever.

LINA. All night. *(Auntie hands out sweets.)*

AUNTIE. A treat for you, Lina. And you. And me. I didn't think you'd be awake.

LINA. Why not? *(Pause.)*

AUNTIE. Girls. We live in an interconnected world. We each play an important but distinct role. All I can do — all I can do is walk you through the worst places. Eat your sweet.

RAHMI. What if I have to pee?

LINA. Don't.

AUNTIE. The salt is good. Cleansing.

LINA. Don't sit.

AUNTIE. You will heal quickly. Won't it be nice finally to command your own body? Tainted gum has lost the war! Don't look at

44

me that way. I've given you the best care I can. I think we could all use sleep. *(Auntie exits.)*

LINA. Doesn't your mouth feel exquisite?

RAHMI. No.

LINA. It will. She's wrong. Gum is pure pleasure.

RAHMI. Gum rots your teeth.

LINA. Gum is for girls.

RAHMI. Gum is rude.

LINA. Gum is modern.

RAHMI. Gum comes wrapped.

LINA. Gum is more than meets the eye.

RAHMI. Gum is sticky.

LINA. But not messy. Gum happens in private.

RAHMI. Gum is a part of your mouth.

LINA. Come to bed.

RAHMI. I think I'm losing blood.

LINA. Walk. *(Lina sings to make Rahmi walk. Loud and strong:)*
    Aiii aiii aiii
    Bird fly so high
    She find the sky and fall down
    Down to ground.

    Why aiii aiii
    She cry aiii aiii
    They watch her die and go down
    Down to ground.

    The world is wide —
    And the rain is sweet
    And my life is an easy day.

    Eeee eeee eeee
    She come to me —
Mother's bracelet.

RAHMI. The doctor gave it back. *(Rahmi shivers. Each "OW" is a single sharp pain.)* OW.

LINA. You're sweating.

RAHMI. It's cold.

LINA. No it's not.

RAHMI. *(Shivers.)* OW. *(Shivers.)* OW. *(Shivers.)* OW.

LINA. Stop it.

RAHMI. I won't be a doctor.

LINA. Yes you will. Walk.

RAHMI. I want music.

LINA. I was thinking about being on a plane with you and seeing the shape of continents. I could talk to the stewardess for both of us and order you juice and candy. You chew gum when the plane takes off for your ears. And then all you do is stay in one exact spot and sleep and eat and watch the person next to you. Me.

RAHMI. Gum.

LINA. I was thinking that on the plane I would bring cloth to spread over your legs against the cold, and slippers for your feet. It will be the cleanest ride of our lives. I imagine your face with sky behind it. When we get to the ground you'll need me just to speak. But you are such a fast learner. Remember how you won the Girls' Prize for scholarship? You knew every number and name by heart. You would chant for an hour, just true things.

I could learn every language in the world and still not know what's true and what's a lie.

RAHMI. Lina.

LINA. For example, did they really remove the source of your wildness and confusion, and if so was it also the source of the funny things you said and your strange loving ways?

And why were we born with extra parts?

RAHMI. Cold.

LINA. Talk louder.

RAHMI. Move to a cold place.

LINA. I'll buy us a ticket. Which one? Siberia and Alaska and Boston and Copenhagen. Which one? *(Rahmi stumbles.)*

RAHMI. Oww.

LINA. Don't you dare.

RAHMI. Hold me? Care me?

LINA. Don't you dare.

RAHMI. *(Shivers.)* Oww. *(Shivers.)* Oww.

LINA. OWW. OWW. Other people have the exact same pain and don't yell about it. Did you ever think that? That hot tea hitting

your skin and mine makes the same exact feeling and you scream and scream and other people don't? It's not like you're the only girl in the world. It hurts. So? Millions of girls hurt just as much.
RAHMI. I can't see.
LINA. Stop it.
RAHMI. They're pinching my eye.
LINA. AUNTIE!
RAHMI. They're squeezing my eye through a strainer and boiling it like grain.
LINA. Talk reasonable. *(Rahmi speaks with sudden clarity.)*
RAHMI. We choose our most precise scalpel. We disinfect it. We strap down the subject's head. We pierce the iris and slash through the suspensor ligaments one by one. We pick out the lens. We cut away the eyeball, reach in and remove it. We peel back the retina and sever the optic nerve. We scrape out the socket. We stuff grass in the wound and tape it closed. We stuff grass in the mouth and tape it closed. *(A terrible hemorrhage. Rahmi faints.)*
LINA. Auntie. AUNTIE! *(Auntie enters.)*
AUNTIE. Like a girl in a village with broken glass. I should have called the ambulance before. *(Auntie exits.)*
LINA. Stop bleeding stop bleeding stop bleeding stop bleeding stop bleeding. *(Lina slaps Rahmi. No response. Slaps harder. No response. She checks for breath. She tries to wake her. Lina realizes Rahmi is dead.)*
　　My big sister.
　　Every stupid thing in the world is breathing except you.
　　Every dumb frog and ugly girl and mean man and poison bug.
　　Every country and river and language and land.
　　Everything.
　　Even me.
　　You do every single thing first.
　　It's not fair.
(Auntie returns.)
AUNTIE. She looks lovely and still. The doctor will wake — *(Realizes.)* And I said she's not bleeding and whoosh.
　　And I looked at her bleeding and said kiss your son.
　　And I said kiss your son. And she kissed you.
　　Lina.

The daughter of watery eyes.

LINA. I was always supposed to be someone else? *(Silence.)*

AUNTIE. Everything was clean and the doctor seemed steady. There should have been no complication.

LINA. Some people are fragile.

AUNTIE. She would cry to get her hair combed.

LINA. Oww. Oww. Lina first, Lina first. Oww. Remember when I cut her braid off and you made me stop eating for two days? She asked me to. She was sick of the pain.

AUNTIE. Did she at least sneak you food?

LINA. She fed me from her hand.

AUNTIE. I smell terrible.

LINA. Help me move her.

AUNTIE. I want to get in that bath and never come out.

LINA. Why do we take hot baths in a hot place?

AUNTIE. Because you can't fight heat.

LINA. Then why do we do this?

AUNTIE. I don't know. *(Lina washes the body. A prayer:)*

When the sun is wrapped up
and the stars fall like rocks
and the mountains go flat
and wild animals stand as one
and oceans boil
and bodies meet souls
and when the baby girl buried alive is asked
what was your crime?
And when all books are opened and the sky peels back
and hell is on fire and heaven is close

And my sister at twenty
wakes and walks
and leads me to a garden of lost parts
where truth runs like blood
and memory stops

Then we will know what we do.

Ten

Three days later. The garden is altered in mourning. Lina is alone. She tries to pray.

Inayat enters unseen. He watches Lina.

INAYAT. Peace on your house.
LINA. AUNTIE! *(Auntie enters.)*
AUNTIE. Lina, bring cigarettes and coffee. *(Lina exits.)* My brother is ill inside.
INAYAT. I'm sorry.
AUNTIE. Actually he doesn't want to see you.
INAYAT. It was a one in a thousand disaster. We sat in your pretty garden and agreed.
AUNTIE. Time has gotten short and long at once.
INAYAT. Yes it has. I've worked every day since I was eight. It feels like a holiday, but empty.
AUNTIE. She was a useless, disagreeable girl. In twenty years she did not do one thing I asked. She was disobedient, disrespectful —
INAYAT. Dishonored.
AUNTIE. Don't insult my child. *(Lina enters, veiled, with a tray.)* Sit on the ground and drink bitter with us. Smoke and clear your head.
INAYAT. What a grand house. This courtyard is open and protected at once. The smell rises away.
LINA. She taught me how to smoke without coughing.
INAYAT. Once I was told to identify the dangerous part of a woman, and remove it. But it wasn't the gum. It wasn't even her body. So this treacherous part of a woman that draws you close, then scrapes off your skin like twenty rough rocks to leave you bloody and raw, is invisible. Invincible. Intact. And I am afraid.

Lina. Good Auntie. The time of sorrow has barely begun. But in these weeks of courtship I have learned to like you — maybe best of all. And now. Certainly. Best of all.

The offer stands.

I would be honored to love this sister.

AUNTIE. Everyone knew about Rahmi. No one would want her but you. Lina has never been kissed by a man. She can find a better match.

INAYAT. I see.

AUNTIE. You pick a bad girl and try to tame her.

INAYAT. You consented.

AUNTIE. Yes I did.

INAYAT. It is not a risky procedure. We chose the most moderate, in a hospital. It was not a primitive thing.

AUNTIE. Some naive women just don't heal.

INAYAT. I love this family.

AUNTIE. Get back to your shop.

INAYAT. *(Stands. A blessing:)*
    By the splendor of dawn
    and the still of dusk
    you are not forgotten, not forsaken.
    And your future will be better than now
    and you will receive, and you will find joy.
    Weren't you once an orphan?
    Weren't you once mistaken?
    Weren't you once poor?
    Remember to hold the orphan.
    Remember to listen to questions.
    Remember to tell the story.
    The story of change.

(Inayat exits.)

AUNTIE. You sit there like a chair.

LINA. It's not my place to talk.

AUNTIE. Most of how I raised you was wrong.

LINA. Oh no. My mother asked you to care just —

AUNTIE. *(Overlapping on "you.")* Your mother thought you were a boy.

LINA. I see.

AUNTIE. I didn't want to disappoint her.

LINA. Then it's true. I'm not really Lina. I'm someone else. She blessed me as someone else.

AUNTIE. You have grown into such a gentle person.

LINA. I watched the ones I admire. Her, and you. I hoped I might learn. I hoped we might grow middle-aged while you grew old. I hoped the strange books I read might make me a little less stupid. But I am only a girl.

AUNTIE. Lina.

LINA. Yes.

AUNTIE. Go away. *(Long silence. Then, slowly:)*

LINA. But here is where the house remembers Rahmi.

AUNTIE. Use her jewelry.

LINA. Your health will fail.

AUNTIE. I will grow old in an old place.

LINA. She bled to death right here.

AUNTIE. You are exactly the child we wanted.

Don't come back.

(Auntie exits. Lina climbs the wall.)

LINA. There are places where rain falls out of season. Where you make a mistake or a footprint, and suddenly see it washed clean.

(Lina goes to a new place.)

End of Play

PROPERTY LIST

Gum (LINA, INAYAT)
Perfume vial (INAYAT)
Cigarettes, lighter (INAYAT)
Tea, cups (LINA, AUNTIE)
Walkman (LINA, AUNTIE)
Books (RAHMI and LINA)
Package of cassettes filled with gum (LINA)
Package of cloth (RAHMI, AUNTIE)
Package of different cloth (LINA)
House of gum wrappers (LINA)
Cane (RAHMI)
Sweets (AUNTIE)
Cigarettes, coffee (LINA)

SOUND EFFECTS

Terrible high-pitched sound

MUSIC

Kim D. Sherman set the songs to gorgeous music, which is strongly suggested for production. The rights may be obtained through Helen Merrill Ltd., 295 Lafayette Street, Suite 915, New York, NY 10012. Tel. (212) 226-5015, Fax (212) 226-5079.

THE MOTHER OF
MODERN CENSORSHIP

This play is dedicated to Mark Bly.

THE MOTHER OF MODERN CENSORHIP was produced at the Yale Cabaret in New Haven, Connecticut, on February 29, 1996. It was directed by Karen Hartman, with sets by Louisa Thompson, costumes by Cristina Desrosiers, lights by Susan Hamburger, sound by Jane Shaw and stage management by Liz Jones. The cast was as follows:

THURAYA AL-GHINDI .... Tessa Auberjonois
SAMIA FAHMI .... Kimberly Ross
KHADIGA SAAD .... Jackeline Duprey
OMAR HAMMOUDA .... Johnny Sparks

THE MOTHER OF MODERN CENSORSHIP was produced at HERE (Barbara Busackino, Kim Maner, Kristin Marting and Randy Rollison, Producing Directors) through Lincoln Center's American Living Room series in New York City on July 18, 1996. It was directed by Leah C. Gardiner, with sets by Daphne Klein, costumes by Ilona Symogyi, lights by Tyler Micoleau, sound by Jill Duboff and stage management by Robert Castro. The cast was as follows:

THURAYA AL-GHINDI .... Mercedes Herrero
SAMIA FAHMI .... Greer Goodman
KHADIGA SAAD .... Meg Brogan
OMAR HAMMOUDA .... Mark H. Dold

THE MOTHER OF MODERN CENSORSHIP received its world premiere at Circle X Theatre Company (Jonathan Westerberg and Jim Anzide, Producing Artistic Directors) in Los Angeles, California, on November 17, 2000. It was directed by Jim Anzide, with sets by Gillian Harwood, costumes by Mara West, lights by Michael E. R. Habicht, sound by Paul Hepker and Jonathan Westerberg and stage management by Rebecca Avery. The cast was as follows:

THURAYA AL-GHINDI .... Jennifer Toffel
SAMIA FAHMI .... Luck Hari
KHADIGA SAAD .... Daniele O'Loughlin
OMAR HAMMOUDA .... Matthew Allen Bretz

CHARACTERS

THURAYA AL-GHINDI — Chief Music Censor, late forties

SAMIA FAHMI — Assistant Music Censor, late forties

KHADIGA SAAD — The New Girl, twenties

OMAR HAMMOUDA — Head of All Censorship, late thirties

SETTING

A cramped office in the Censorship Headquarters of a fictitious country.

TIME

The present.

NOTE

THE MOTHER OF MODERN CENSORSHIP takes place in a fictional country and may be performed by actors of any race or ethnicity, in any combination.

THE MOTHER OF MODERN CENSORSHIP

A cramped office with a row of three desks. Thuraya al-Ghindi, Chief Music Censor, sits stage right. Thuraya is in her late forties; she wears a long skirt but her hair is uncovered. At the middle desk sits Samia Fahmi, Thuraya's assistant. Samia is the same age as Thuraya; she wears a more conservative robe, as well as a head-scarf and gloves. The third desk is empty. On each desk is a boom box and a set of headphones, with a trash can to the left. There is a pile of cassette tapes on Thuraya's desk and another pile on the empty desk. At rise, Thuraya and Samia are both listening with headphones. The women stop their tapes at the same time, eject them, and set them on the desk to their left: Thuraya on Samia's desk, Samia on the empty desk. Thuraya inserts a new tape from her pile. Samia inserts the tape she just got from Thuraya and rewinds it. The women listen. Again, they stop the tapes. Samia places her tape on the empty desk; Thuraya throws her tape in the trash, puts in a new tape, and listens. Samia sits at her empty desk, doing nothing. Thuraya ejects the tape, throws it in the trash, inserts another tape and listens for a long time, perhaps tapping her fingers to the music. Samia waits. Nothing. Samia sneaks a tape out of Thuraya's trash can and puts it in her own tape player. The women listen. Thuraya notices that Samia, too, is listening to music. Thuraya takes off her headphones and looks at Samia. Samia does not respond.

THURAYA. It is a reject. *(No response. Thuraya stops Samia's tape player.)* It is a reject.
SAMIA. I'm not so sure. *(Samia starts her tape again. Thuraya puts on her headphones. The women listen. Thuraya takes off her headphones and stops her tape.)*
THURAYA. You don't have to be sure.
SAMIA. Hmm? *(Thuraya stops Samia's tape.)*

THURAYA. You don't have to be sure. Nobody cares if you're sure. If one of us is sure, then we as a decision-making force are sure.

SAMIA. I know how it works, Thuraya.

THURAYA. You should.

SAMIA. After seventeen years I should.

THURAYA. I too know how it works, Samia.

SAMIA. You should.

THURAYA. After half my son's lifetime I should. And after my granddaughter's lifetime in charge, I should.

SAMIA. We know how it works.

THURAYA. So why is it that after I, Thuraya al-Ghindi, Chief Music Censor, have rejected a certain piece of music you pull it out of the trash and proceed to pretend to judge it?

SAMIA. Because, Thuraya, there is nothing else to do.

THURAYA. That is a serious problem.

SAMIA. A person comes to work to do a job.

THURAYA. A person comes to work to earn a living.

SAMIA. A person of a certain security level with a certain kind of employed husband comes to work to use what talents she may have, to give back to her culture.

THURAYA. You are a noble woman, Samia Fahmi.

SAMIA. Our work is vital.

THURAYA. So why don't you let me do it?

SAMIA. Because I don't trust you.

THURAYA. Do you lack faith in Mr. Omar Hammouda, Head of All Censorship —

SAMIA. I know Mr. Hammouda —

THURAYA. — who appointed me to this position?

SAMIA. The Chief Music Censor should be a person of high reputation, good family and clear faith.

THURAYA. I am sure we could find something for you to do, if that is the problem. Would you like something to do?

SAMIA. The Chief Music Censor should be a person whose modesty and devotion are plain to see.

THURAYA. The Chief Music Censor should be a person of conviction.

SAMIA. She should listen carefully.

THURAYA. She should not be influenced.

SAMIA. Like Rahmi. *(Both women look at the empty desk. Pause.)*
THURAYA. You could make this office more decorative. You could make this office more stylish. You could make this office more clean.
SAMIA. There you go.
THURAYA. What?
SAMIA. Clean.
THURAYA. What?
SAMIA. Clean.
THURAYA. Try to be lucid, Samia.
SAMIA. I would have to get dirty to make our office clean. I would have to buy supplies from a filthy vendor, then bend over with rags and a bucket and scrub —
THURAYA. You don't scrub with a rag. You wipe. You mop.
SAMIA. I don't know much about it.
THURAYA. Then listen. To scrub requires a scrubbing brush, or other implement. With a rag one might wipe a spill. One might push the rag with a handle and mop a floor, but one would not call this —
SAMIA. You're confusing me.
THURAYA. You could understand housework if you tried.
SAMIA. I didn't want to talk about housework.
THURAYA. My apologies.
SAMIA. I was only talking about housework because you brought up housework —
THURAYA. I was trying to be helpful.
SAMIA.   — and thinking about dirt reminded me of you.
THURAYA. You had requested something to do.
SAMIA. I don't want anything to do anymore.
THURAYA. Then you won't mind if I get back to my job.
SAMIA. It's my job, too.
THURAYA. Well I am sure you're eager for me to continue, so that when there is an appropriate work for you to judge, I can pass it along with due speed. *(Thuraya puts on her headphones and starts the tape.)*
SAMIA. Thuraya? *(No answer.)* Thuraya? *(Samia stops Thuraya's tape. Thuraya removes her headphones.)* What if the new girl doesn't like me?

61

THURAYA. Don't ever do that.

SAMIA. I was just thinking.

THURAYA. How am I supposed to come to a decision if you do that?

SAMIA. I wanted to ask before she gets here.

THURAYA. I am sure the new girl will like you perfectly well if you allow her to get on with her job.

SAMIA. And will she respect me?

THURAYA. Everyone respects you, Samia.

SAMIA. Yes?

THURAYA. You are a respectable woman.

SAMIA. I don't know if that's what I mean.

THURAYA. Well when you think of what you mean be sure to let me know.

SAMIA. All right.

THURAYA. When I come to a natural break in my work.

SAMIA. You haven't worn the veil in five weeks.

THURAYA. Oh.

SAMIA. That's what I mean ... that's what I meant by the floor.

THURAYA. You are insinuating that just as you should become dirty in what would doubtless be a ridiculous effort on your part to clean our floor, I have been sullied, in a moral sense, by the stream of filth which it is my duty to purify.

SAMIA. Yes.

THURAYA. That's a sophisticated hypothesis.

SAMIA. Thank you.

THURAYA. In fact ...

SAMIA. Yes?

THURAYA. In truth ...

SAMIA. Yes?

THURAYA. I cast off the veil because it interferes with my work.

SAMIA. Oh.

THURAYA. Headphones are much more convenient over ears.

SAMIA. I see.

THURAYA. I am trying to become as efficient as possible.

SAMIA. Of course.

THURAYA. So that when the Tower is built I will be able to accommodate the new volume of material.

SAMIA. Oh, the Tower.

THURAYA. It will be superior when we have the Tower.

SAMIA. I will enjoy a comfortable chair and the best headphones.

THURAYA. No headphones, Samia.

SAMIA. No?

THURAYA. Private listening chambers.

SAMIA. Right.

THURAYA. Don't you remember Mr. Hammouda telling us about private listening chambers?

SAMIA. Now I remember. And remote control. And windows.

THURAYA. Our days together are numbered.

SAMIA. That they are! *(Thuraya reaches for her headphones.)* What will we tell the new girl about Rahmi?

THURAYA. The truth.

SAMIA. We will?

THURAYA. If she asks.

SAMIA. We will?

THURAYA. That Rahmi was working here, and now she no longer works here.

SAMIA. That's true. But it's not much of the truth.

THURAYA. We decide how much truth.

SAMIA. Enough so it's true, but not enough so it's harmful.

THURAYA. Exactly.

SAMIA. Rahmi would have enjoyed a private listening chamber.

THURAYA. Stop talking about Rahmi.

SAMIA. You liked her.

THURAYA. Samia Fahmi.

SAMIA. You liked her work. Progressive, you called it.

THURAYA. I meant that in the worst possible sense.

SAMIA. And her own compositions —

THURAYA. STOP!

SAMIA. Rahmi stopped wearing the veil six weeks ago.

THURAYA. Oh.

SAMIA. So.

THURAYA. So it's clear, you think.

SAMIA. I never said clear.

THURAYA. When does clarity ever come to you? But you implied —

63

SAMIA. I stated the truth.

THURAYA. Which truth?

SAMIA. That you used to cover your hands and now you don't even cover your hair.

THURAYA. I never owed you an explanation, yet I gave one.

SAMIA. Partial.

THURAYA. How do you know?

SAMIA. Everything is partial with you. A person doesn't know where she stands. A person starts to forget who she is.

THURAYA. That person can work on remembering when the citizens are not paying for her time.

SAMIA. I want to switch desks.

THURAYA. Do you?

SAMIA. I can listen first, and pass the music to you.

THURAYA. You would like that.

SAMIA. It would reduce your burden.

THURAYA. You think I am not bearing the burden gracefully …

SAMIA. Your job is delicate.

THURAYA. … appropriately.

SAMIA. We could share the initial impact. You would still be Chief Music Censor, of course.

THURAYA. You think I am keeping the gates with reduced vigilance.

SAMIA. I never said that.

THURAYA. Well fuck you, Samia Fahmi. *(Khadiga Saad opens the door and stands in the doorway. Khadiga is in her twenties. She wears a traditional robe, a head scarf, no gloves and lots of gold jewelry.)*

KHADIGA. Mr. Hammouda said to walk right in. Mr. Hammouda said not to knock. Mr. Hammouda said he would have come to introduce me but he is occupied. So I am to introduce myself.

THURAYA. Well.

SAMIA. Introduce yourself.

KHADIGA. I am the new girl. My name is Khadiga Saad. I am very excited about a career in music censorship and I hope that my work will be worthy and respectable. I would like very much to be the conscience of society for a long time to come. I hope I am not in the wrong office. I would like very much to know what to do.

THURAYA. Get out of the doorway.

SAMIA. You have your own desk, Miss Saad.

KHADIGA. Mrs.

SAMIA. Congratulations.

KHADIGA. Thank you.

SAMIA. I am Mrs. Samia Fahmi.

KHADIGA. Congratulations.

SAMIA. This is Thuraya al-Ghindi.

KHADIGA. It is an honor to finally meet you, Mrs. al-Ghindi. I have heard your praises all my life.

THURAYA. I still maintain a high reputation among most people.

KHADIGA. Without you, what would we hear?

THURAYA. I am considered impeccable. Impervious.

SAMIA. We listen to music and decide what could be damaging for society and young people. If something is damaging, we throw it away.

KHADIGA. I see.

THURAYA. Any questions?

KHADIGA. No. Yes.

SAMIA. Yes?

KHADIGA. I feel obliged to point out that I myself am a young person.

SAMIA. True.

THURAYA. Very true.

SAMIA. Only partly true. You see, Mrs. Saad, you are a married woman. So while your years may be limited, you have a certain kind of knowledge —

KHADIGA. Oh.

THURAYA. — which is precisely the kind of knowledge that could damage a person.

KHADIGA. Yes?

SAMIA. So while you are a young person, you are no longer a young girl.

KHADIGA. Already?

THURAYA. Already.

KHADIGA. It will broaden my horizons to work with you.

THURAYA. Sit there.

SAMIA. And when we pass you a piece of music, make a decision.

KHADIGA. Oh goodness.

THURAYA. Get ready, Mrs. Saad. *(Thuraya and Samia put on headphones and listen. Khadiga folds her hands and sits at attention at her desk. Thuraya and Samia eject their tapes at the same time. Thuraya passes her tape to Samia; Samia throws her tape in the trash. Thuraya and Samia listen. Khadiga looks around the office. Thuraya and Samia eject their tapes at the same time and both throw them in the trash. Thuraya puts in a new tape. Samia turns to Khadiga.)*
SAMIA. It will be more pleasant now that there are three again, because you will chat with me while Thuraya is occupied.
KHADIGA. I will like that. I will like also to watch both of you work. Are there special standards to be used?
SAMIA. Oh yes.
KHADIGA. Will I learn what they are?
SAMIA. Mr. Hammouda didn't teach you the checklists?
KHADIGA. Mr. Hammouda didn't have time.
SAMIA. There are checklists.
KHADIGA. Shouldn't Mrs. al-Ghindi be the one to train me?
SAMIA. Mrs. al-Ghindi is occupied.
KHADIGA. You look like an upright person. I shouldn't mind learning from you.
SAMIA. That is a lovely head scarf.
KHADIGA. You too. A lovely head scarf, Mrs. Fahmi. *(Thuraya ejects her tape and passes it to Samia.)*
SAMIA. *(To Khadiga.)* Sorry. *(Samia inserts the tape. Thuraya inserts a new tape. The women listen. Khadiga sits happily at her desk. Some time passes. Khadiga tries to listen by leaning toward Samia's headphones. Thuraya and Samia stop their tapes; each passes to the left. There is now a tape on Khadiga's desk.)*
KHADIGA. Oh goodness. *(Each woman inserts her new tape. Khadiga is about to put on the headphones.)*
SAMIA. She doesn't have the checklist.
THURAYA. No list?
SAMIA. No time, he says.
THURAYA. Well you can't just listen.
KHADIGA. Oh no.
THURAYA. Don't look at me and say, "Oh no," when you were about to just listen.
KHADIGA. I want to do an excellent job as censor.

THURAYA. Don't change the subject.

KHADIGA. I thought that was the subject. My qualifications as censor.

SAMIA. She's right. That was the subject.

THURAYA. Here is our checklist. Any questions?

KHADIGA. No. Yes. Rate from one to ten the following: offensiveness of language, ungodliness of tone, allusion to lewd acts. What are lewd acts?

THURAYA. Lewd: obscene, vulgar, inappropriate, suggestive.

SAMIA. Forbidden.

KHADIGA. Forbidden acts. Is one the highest or the lowest?

THURAYA. Highest.   SAMIA. Lowest.

THURAYA. Don't confuse her. One is the highest in tone.

SAMIA. The most offensive receives a ten.

KHADIGA. Rate from one to five: troubling Western influence, troubling northern influence, troubling revolutionary influence. Revolutionary?

SAMIA. Secularists.   THURAYA. Fundamentalists.

KHADIGA. All right then.

THURAYA. Go to.

KHADIGA. Oh goodness. *(All three women listen to tapes. Thuraya and Samia eject their tapes and pass them to the left. Khadiga continues to listen, becoming more and more audibly aroused. Thuraya and Samia remove their headphones.)*

SAMIA. Mrs. Saad?

THURAYA. We have work to do.

SAMIA. Mrs. Saad.

THURAYA. Remove her headphones. *(Samia does.)*

SAMIA. Mrs. Saad?

KHADIGA. I've never heard anything like this.

SAMIA and THURAYA. No?

KHADIGA. Not on the radio, not on the television, not anywhere in public.

SAMIA and THURAYA. Oh.

KHADIGA. What rating did you give?

SAMIA. Thuraya approved it.

THURAYA. We each approved it.

SAMIA. But, Thuraya, as Chief Music Censor, knows why.

THURAYA. Cassette 8-4-3-B-F-6-9. Offensiveness of language: none. One. Ungodliness of tone: no godliness, but no particular ungodliness. Two and a half. Allusion to lewd acts —

KHADIGA. Yes.

THURAYA. What was your lewd acts mark?

SAMIA. Two.

THURAYA. There is no reference to a man in the song.

SAMIA. There is no reference to an act.

THURAYA. Western influence? Northern influence? Revolutionary influence?

SAMIA. No, no, no.

SAMIA and THURAYA. Mrs. Saad, could the smut be in your head?

KHADIGA. The way she breathes is not something I have heard in public.

THURAYA. If a woman is not allowed to breathe —

SAMIA. Let's listen again.

THURAYA. I don't have time to listen to each selection twice due to lack of consensus. *(Samia inserts the tape and puts on her headphones.)*

KHADIGA. I concede.

THURAYA. Samia. *(No response.)*

KHADIGA. Or I will concede, once you explain the category for breathing like that.

THURAYA. Samia. *(No response. To Khadiga.)* You have had an influence. Mrs. Fahmi is going to remove those headphones and reverse her decision. That is why we need the Tower.

KHADIGA. Oh yes.

THURAYA. You don't know anything about the Tower.

KHADIGA. The Tower will hold private listening chambers and a range of comfortable furniture. All technology will be modern. It will overlook the river and our tallest cultural buildings.

THURAYA. That is classified information.

KHADIGA. Within the Tower, censorship will become a learned profession under the Censorship Development Plan. Training programs for future censors will be incorporated into the Academy of Fine Arts.

THURAYA. I have not heard that.

KHADIGA. I know.

THURAYA. And I am Chief Music Censor.

KHADIGA. Did you think our profession would remain unregulated in this advanced age?

SAMIA. Oh. Oh! OH!

THURAYA. Quit it.

SAMIA. Her breathing is unusual. *(Samia takes off the headphones.)* Thuraya, you have to hear this breathing.

THURAYA. I heard the selection.

SAMIA. It is unmistakable, uncivil, subversive.

THURAYA. I approved of the selection.

SAMIA. There is some dissent.

KHADIGA. Perhaps as Mrs. al-Ghindi has listened to so much music on so many levels over so many years, she does not notice such breathing on a first round.

THURAYA. I notice everything.

SAMIA. Perhaps as Mrs. al-Ghindi is no longer married, such sounds are less familiar.

KHADIGA. Perhaps such sounds are very familiar. Perhaps Mrs. al-Ghindi makes such sounds every day.

THURAYA. Suck my dick. *(Thuraya puts on the headphones and inserts the cassette.)*

SAMIA. I am surprised by you.

KHADIGA. I'm sorry.

SAMIA. You seemed like a very naive young person and now you behave in a way which is surprising.

KHADIGA. I am a naive young person. I surprise myself.

SAMIA. You told Thuraya you have heard her praises all your life. You addressed us both with respect, but showed a preference for her. And now you make hurtful and rude remarks.

KHADIGA. My respect is for Mrs. al-Ghindi's central role in the field of censorship. Perhaps because of this awe, I hold her to a higher standard.

SAMIA. We all do.

KHADIGA. Is it your experience that Mrs. al-Ghindi consistently meets the moral requirements of Chief Music Censor?

THURAYA. *(Without removing headphones.)* I see two tapes on two desks and a clock which is ticking. *(Samia and Khadiga insert tapes and put on headphones. Khadiga discreetly unplugs first her own headphones, then Samia's. She speaks to Samia while facing forward, as if still listening.)*

KHADIGA. Or do you have doubts?

SAMIA. Thuraya and I have worked side by side for seventeen years.

KHADIGA. And?

SAMIA. After seven of those years, she was promoted to Chief Music Censor. I remained Assistant.

KHADIGA. And?

SAMIA. For ten years I accede to her judgment, as do the citizens of this country.

KHADIGA. Whom am I replacing?

SAMIA. A lady named Rahmi.

KHADIGA. What happened to Rahmi?

SAMIA. Rahmi used to work here and now she no longer works here.

KHADIGA. That is incomplete information.

SAMIA. I am only Assistant.

KHADIGA. So far.

SAMIA. Sorry? *(Thuraya removes her headphones.)*

THURAYA. I suppose deep breathing is a deep offense.

SAMIA. If even one of us rejects a selection, it is eliminated.

THURAYA. Why can you hear me?

SAMIA. You speak clearly and well? *(Thuraya sees that the womens' headphones are unplugged.)*

THURAYA. I will not be discussed. I am not on the table for discussion. Is that understood?

SAMIA. Yes.

KHADIGA. Oh yes.

THURAYA. I am Chief Music Censor and when I place headphones over ears to do my job, it is critical to know I am not being discussed. So Miss Khadiga if you cannot join forces with our enterprise I suggest you seek employment elsewhere.

KHADIGA. I have been hired here.

THURAYA. I should not like to request a word with Mr. Hammouda.

SAMIA. Won't it be nice in the Tower when we can hear our

music without seeing each other's faces? Why don't we all have a nice listen and a nice think about the Tower.

THURAYA. Not everyone will be invited to the Tower.

KHADIGA. Finally some true information.

THURAYA. For seventeen years I have listened to lyrics depicting acts and ideas which do not even have names in our language. It is my duty to comprehend this information, sift through it, and eliminate what could rot our moral and family system while maintaining some connection to the modern world. Is it true information? I am not sure. I have not traveled. But it is volatile information, important information, exclusive information, and I am its sole recipient.

KHADIGA. Who knew about the training program?

SAMIA. I'm going to be ahead of you ladies if we don't all get back to work. *(Samia puts on her headphones.)*

THURAYA. I don't believe in such a program.

KHADIGA. I don't believe in some of the activities which take place in your songs. And yet they exist.

THURAYA. Tell me what you know.

KHADIGA. I am not an informationally privileged person. I am applying as a common student. I have merely read the forms.

THURAYA. There are forms?

KHADIGA. With help from above, I will receive a higher degree in Censorship as a Fine Art.

THURAYA. The Tower is on these forms?

KHADIGA. My husband has an inside job.

THURAYA. You know more than you let on.

KHADIGA. It is my goal to be well educated.

THURAYA. You chose the right field.

KHADIGA. In my marriage contract I specified that I be allowed to continue my learning, but did not indicate in what. After the wedding my husband said he would be most comfortable if I pursued study in the field of censorship. I am grateful for this position. I doubt many other applicants will have practical experience.

THURAYA. You speak as though these developments have no bearing upon me. *(Samia takes off her headphones.)*

SAMIA. Someone should do some work around here.

THURAYA. I set the schedule.

SAMIA. Enjoy that while you can.

THURAYA. I run this office. And you are Assistant.

SAMIA. So far. Hmm? So far.

KHADIGA. Change is inevitable.

SAMIA. The question is, which way?

THURAYA. Stop being slippery. I will not tolerate slipperiness.

SAMIA. After seventeen years I don't know who you are.

THURAYA. Do you want to change desks again?

SAMIA. In the Tower I will paint my new office blue to remind me of sky.

THURAYA. There will be windows.

SAMIA. I don't think I will have time to look out the windows. Or the need. If everything is blue like the sky, even the telephone, I won't want to daydream. My large large office on the top floor.

THURAYA. *(To Khadiga.)* Have you told her something I don't know?

SAMIA. The very top floor.

THURAYA. The top floor will be given to the top position. I have the top position but now we all sit on one level due to the economic necessity of insufficient grandeur. In the Tower, she who hears most will have the broadest vision.

SAMIA. You're right so far. Hmm? So far.

THURAYA. I will need more space and more light in my working quarters once my title expands to include Professor.

SAMIA. Professor. Hah!

THURAYA. Perhaps Mrs. Saad did not inform you that my system of censor education is to take shape as a program of higher learning, with myself top and center.

SAMIA. She? *(Khadiga is at Thuraya's desk, looking through the tapes.)*

KHADIGA. I know very little.

SAMIA. You are so confident about expansion, Thuraya al-Ghindi. Since the day I met you you have been so very very certain of yourself. If a Tower is built, you will naturally rise to occupy it, hmm? And poor Samia will bring your tea in an elevator. Poor modest Samia will push the buttons and wipe the mirrors on this elevator. That will be the benefit of the Tower to poor pampered Samia. She will learn a little duty. She will gain a little gruffness to match your own working-class roots.

THURAYA. Not working class.

KHADIGA. But you have worked since you were twelve, supporting first your mother, then your children, and when your son abandoned them, your grandchildren.

THURAYA. Why do you know facts about my life? Why are you sitting at my desk?

KHADIGA. You are the most powerful woman in the country. *(Khadiga slips on Thuraya's headphones.)*

THURAYA. Remove them. REMOVE THEM.

KHADIGA. Get ready, Mrs. Fahmi.

SAMIA. Oh yes. *(Samia sits at her desk.)* Why am I exactly where I started?

KHADIGA. There is no significance in the order of the desks.

SAMIA. Oh.

THURAYA. I'm not sitting there.

KHADIGA. We don't have a selection for you yet anyway.

SAMIA. You can wait nicely. *(Samia and Khadiga insert tapes and begin to listen.)*

THURAYA. Usurped. Usurped. *(Thuraya unplugs Samia's and Khadiga's headphones from the tape players and grabs them. She wields the cords like a whip.)* I AM THE MOTHER OF MODERN CENSORSHIP! *(Thuraya knocks all the tapes to the ground. Samia puts her hands over her ears.)*

SAMIA. She is an unpredictable person, an easily influenced person, not my sort of person at all.

THURAYA. Get your hands off your ears, Samia Fahmi. Together we have built a system. Now she sits at my desk.

KHADIGA. No one can expose herself to a disease and remain unafflicted. *(Thuraya cracks the cord/whip on the desk, close to Khadiga.)*

THURAYA. Up you young thing, you think-you're-strong thing.

KHADIGA. I have always argued that you are still fit for your job.

THURAYA. UP!

KHADIGA. I have no weapon.

THURAYA. You are a weapon.

KHADIGA. I won't sink —

THURAYA. Oh, but you will. Even in the Tower, you will. Up. Up. UP! *(Thuraya cracks the whip on the desk. Khadiga drops to the ground and starts collecting the spilled tapes. Samia pulls her veil over her eyes.)*

SAMIA. What I see and hear flows through me like a river leaving no trace.

KHADIGA. Old poisoned thing!

THURAYA. Vicious backbiting cunt! *(Omar Hammouda enters. He is in his late thirties and elegantly dressed.)*

HAMMOUDA. Ladies.

SAMIA. It's good to see you, Mr. Hammouda.

HAMMOUDA. You can't see me at all.

SAMIA. Clever.

HAMMOUDA. Why don't we take off our veil and look at the situation?

THURAYA. Are you wearing a veil?

SAMIA. Thuraya.

HAMMOUDA. Pardon?

THURAYA. You said "we." Are you sporting a new fashion?

HAMMOUDA. Why have you taken the headsets hostage?

THURAYA. Only a person can be a hostage. *(Khadiga starts to cry.)*

HAMMOUDA. You have beaten our new girl into the ground.

KHADIGA. I wanted to do a nice job.

HAMMOUDA. Comfort, Samia? *(Samia crawls to Khadiga without removing her veil.)*

THURAYA. *(To Samia.)* Stop averting your eyes.

HAMMOUDA. Why are you bullwhipping my staff?

THURAYA. Only the desks, Hammouda.

HAMMOUDA. Please refer —

THURAYA. How old were you seventeen years ago?

HAMMOUDA. You have been granted an unusual degree of power.

THURAYA. Young enough to be my son's friend. Which you were not.

HAMMOUDA. I came to inspect the new girl's progress. I had hoped you were up to the task of educating her.

THURAYA. Educating! Talk to me about educating. *(Thuraya snaps her whip.)*

74

HAMMOUDA. Are you having hormonal trouble?

THURAYA. I'll beat you back and tie you down and shove that crocodile shoe up your ass.

HAMMOUDA. I'll have you shot. *(Pause.)* Can we talk like civilized beings?

THURAYA. Quite. *(Pause.)* I understand the Tower will contain elements not previously discussed with Mrs. Fahmi or myself.

HAMMOUDA. Such as?

THURAYA. A school.

HAMMOUDA. That's classified information.

THURAYA. Forms have been printed.

HAMMOUDA. But not distributed. *(Khadiga squeals in terror.)*

THURAYA. How I obtained the information ceases to be a matter of concern.

HAMMOUDA. It is true that a training program for future censors will be incorporated into the Academy of Fine Arts.

THURAYA. Who will administer this program?

HAMMOUDA. We feel that censorship as it is practiced today is sufficiently far-reaching and noble to fill the present building, and we commend your achievement. However as our quarters expand, the breadth, depth and glory of our faculty must incrementally grow.

THURAYA. Who?

HAMMOUDA. Experts have been invited.

THURAYA. What about Mrs. Fahmi and myself?

HAMMOUDA. You will be fascinated by the innovations. Vague categories such as "allusion to lewd acts" may be replaced by gauges from one to one hundred on a variety of adjectives. Also, censors will be trained to count the number of offenses, rather than arriving at a subjective rating. Furthermore, in the final year of training students will learn to create new categories of offense, ensuring that the system will be flexible as well as precise. None of these ideas have been released to the public, as the experts are still formulating. But I know you can keep a secret.

THURAYA. What will be our role in the new administration?

HAMMOUDA. I understand you are reaching a time of biological change, an age at which many women prefer to go away and never be heard from again.

THURAYA. Is that your preference, Samia?

SAMIA. I got a job because there is work to be done.

HAMMOUDA. In which case you are invited to apply as students.

THURAYA. Students.

SAMIA. Thuraya has been Chief Music Censor for a decade. She knows more dirty words than anyone in the land.

HAMMOUDA. When a system changes, knowledge becomes obsolete.

SAMIA. Thuraya is the most contemporary citizen of all.

HAMMOUDA. If we want our field to develop, we cannot leave it in the hands of women. *(Khadiga stands.)*

KHADIGA. I see that my ambition is in vain. *(Khadiga exits.)*

HAMMOUDA. She's one of our brightest prospects.

THURAYA. Better catch her.

HAMMOUDA. The degree will carry prestige. Consider it. *(Hammouda exits. Silence. Samia picks up a set of headphones off the ground, carries it to her desk and prepares a tape for listening.)*

THURAYA. They will pay someone to re-check our work.

SAMIA. You are the smartest person I have ever known.

THURAYA. Never worship.

SAMIA. Bastard. Motherfucker.

THURAYA. Every insult comes back to us.

SAMIA. I quit! Right now. I'm not waiting to be notified. I'm not going for any degree, even if classes are held on the top floor. If it's not our Tower, I shall never set foot inside! *(Pause.)* Are you coming, friend? *(Thuraya surveys her wrecked domain, cassettes scattered everywhere.)*

THURAYA. Take as many as you like. *(Samia first scoops up one, then grabs several more tapes. She exits, grabbing the tape player on her way out. Thuraya inserts a tape into her tape player. The forbidden music blares at full volume. Thuraya dances. Lights fade.)*

End of Play

PROPERTY LIST

Three boom boxes
Three sets of headphones
Pile of cassette tapes
Checklist (THURAYA)

SOUND EFFECTS

Loud music (e.g., feisty female rap)

NEW PLAYS

★ **MONTHS ON END by Craig Pospisil.** In comic scenes, one for each month of the year, we follow the intertwined worlds of a circle of friends and family whose lives are poised between happiness and heartbreak. "...a triumph...these twelve vignettes all form crucial pieces in the eternal puzzle known as human relationships, an area in which the playwright displays an assured knowledge that spans deep sorrow to unbounded happiness." *–Ann Arbor News.* "...rings with emotional truth, humor...[an] endearing contemplation on love...entertaining and satisfying." *–Oakland Press.* [5M, 5W] ISBN: 0-8222-1892-5

★ **GOOD THING by Jessica Goldberg.** Brings us into the households of John and Nancy Roy, forty-something high-school guidance counselors whose marriage has been increasingly on the rocks and Dean and Mary, recent graduates struggling to make their way in life. "...a blend of gritty social drama, poetic humor and unsubtle existential contemplation..." *–Variety.* [3M, 3W] ISBN: 0-8222-1869-0

★ **THE DEAD EYE BOY by Angus MacLachlan.** Having fallen in love at their Narcotics Anonymous meeting, Billy and Shirley-Diane are striving to overcome the past together. But their relationship is complicated by the presence of Sorin, Shirley-Diane's fourteen-year-old son, a damaged reminder of her dark past. "...a grim, insightful portrait of an unmoored family..." *–NY Times.* "MacLachlan's play isn't for the squeamish, but then, tragic stories delivered at such an unrelenting fever pitch rarely are." *–Variety.* [1M, 1W, 1 boy] ISBN: 0-8222-1844-5

★ **[SIC] by Melissa James Gibson.** In adjacent apartments three young, ambitious neighbors come together to discuss, flirt, argue, share their dreams and plan their futures with unequal degrees of deep hopefulness and abject despair. "A work...concerned with the sound and power of language..." *–NY Times.* "...a wonderfully original take on urban friendship and the comedy of manners—a *Design for Living* for our times..." *–NY Observer.* [3M, 2W] ISBN: 0-8222-1872-0

★ **LOOKING FOR NORMAL by Jane Anderson.** Roy and Irma's twenty-five-year marriage is thrown into turmoil when Roy confesses that he is actually a woman trapped in a man's body, forcing the couple to wrestle with the meaning of their marriage and the delicate dynamics of family. "Jane Anderson's bittersweet transgender domestic comedy-drama ...is thoughtful and touching and full of wit and wisdom. A real audience pleaser." *–Hollywood Reporter.* [5M, 4W] ISBN: 0-8222-1857-7

★ **ENDPAPERS by Thomas McCormack.** The regal Joshua Maynard, the old and ailing head of a mid-sized, family-owned book-publishing house in New York City, must name a successor. One faction in the house backs a smart, "pragmatic" manager, the other faction a smart, "sensitive" editor and both factions fear what the other's man could do to this house— and to them. "If Kaufman and Hart had undertaken a comedy about the publishing business, they might have written *Endpapers*...a breathlessly fast, funny, and thoughtful comedy ...keeps you amused, guessing, and often surprised...profound in its empathy for the paradoxes of human nature." *–NY Magazine.* [7M, 4W] ISBN: 0-8222-1908-5

★ **THE PAVILION by Craig Wright.** By turns poetic and comic, romantic and philosophical, this play asks old lovers to face the consequences of difficult choices made long ago. "The script's greatest strength lies in the genuineness of its feeling." *–Houston Chronicle.* "Wright's perceptive, gently witty writing makes this familiar situation fresh and thoroughly involving." *–Philadelphia Inquirer.* [2M, 1W (flexible casting)] ISBN: 0-8222-1898-4

DRAMATISTS PLAY SERVICE, INC.
440 Park Avenue South, New York, NY 10016 212-683-8960 Fax 212-213-1539
postmaster@dramatists.com www.dramatists.com

NEW PLAYS

★ **BE AGGRESSIVE by Annie Weisman.** Vista Del Sol is paradise, sandy beaches, avocado-lined streets. But for seventeen-year-old cheerleader Laura, everything changes when her mother is killed in a car crash, and she embarks on a journey to the Spirit Institute of the South where she can learn "cheer" with Bible belt intensity. "...filled with lingual gymnastics...stylized rapid-fire dialogue..." *–Variety.* "...a new, exciting, and unique voice in the American theatre..." *–BackStage West.* [1M, 4W, extras] ISBN: 0-8222-1894-1

★ **FOUR by Christopher Shinn.** Four people struggle desperately to connect in this quiet, sophisticated, moving drama. "...smart, broken-hearted...Mr. Shinn has a precocious and forgiving sense of how power shifts in the game of sexual pursuit...He promises to be a playwright to reckon with..." *–NY Times.* "A voice emerges from an American place. It's got humor, sadness and a fresh and touching rhythm that tell of the loneliness and secrets of life...[a] poetic, haunting play." *–NY Post.* [3M, 1W] ISBN: 0-8222-1850-X

★ **WONDER OF THE WORLD by David Lindsay-Abaire.** A madcap picaresque involving Niagara Falls, a lonely tour-boat captain, a pair of bickering private detectives and a husband's dirty little secret. "Exceedingly whimsical and playfully wicked. Winning and genial. A top-drawer production." *–NY Times.* "Full frontal lunacy is on display. A most assuredly fresh and hilarious tragicomedy of marital discord run amok...absolutely hysterical..." *–Variety.* [3M, 4W (doubling)] ISBN: 0-8222-1863-1

★ **QED by Peter Parnell.** Nobel Prize-winning physicist and all-around genius Richard Feynman holds forth with captivating wit and wisdom in this fascinating biographical play that originally starred Alan Alda. "QED is a seductive mix of science, human affections, moral courage, and comic eccentricity. It reflects on, among other things, death, the absence of God, travel to an unexplored country, the pleasures of drumming, and the need to know and understand." *–NY Magazine.* "Its rhythms correspond to the way that people—even geniuses—approach and avoid highly emotional issues, and it portrays Feynman with affection and awe." *–The New Yorker.* [1M, 1W] ISBN: 0-8222-1924-7

★ **UNWRAP YOUR CANDY by Doug Wright.** Alternately chilling and hilarious, this deliciously macabre collection of four bedtime tales for adults is guaranteed to keep you awake for nights on end. "Engaging and intellectually satisfying...a treat to watch." *–NY Times.* "Fiendishly clever. Mordantly funny and chilling. Doug Wright teases, freezes and zaps us." *–Village Voice.* "Four bite-size plays that bite back." *–Variety.* [flexible casting] ISBN: 0-8222-1871-2

★ **FURTHER THAN THE FURTHEST THING by Zinnie Harris.** On a remote island in the middle of the Atlantic secrets are buried. When the outside world comes calling, the islanders find their world blown apart from the inside as well as beyond. "Harris winningly produces an intimate and poetic, as well as political, family saga." *–Independent (London).* "Harris' enthralling adventure of a play marks a departure from stale, well-furrowed theatrical terrain." *–Evening Standard (London).* [3M, 2W] ISBN: 0-8222-1874-7

★ **THE DESIGNATED MOURNER by Wallace Shawn.** The story of three people living in a country where what sort of books people like to read and how they choose to amuse themselves becomes both firmly personal and unexpectedly entangled with questions of survival. "This is a playwright who does not just tell you what it is like to be arrested at night by goons or to fall morally apart and become an aimless yet weirdly contented ghost yourself. He has the originality to make you feel it." *–Times (London).* "A fascinating play with beautiful passages of writing..." *–Variety.* [2M, 1W] ISBN: 0-8222-1848-8

DRAMATISTS PLAY SERVICE, INC.
440 Park Avenue South, New York, NY 10016 212-683-8960 Fax 212-213-1539
postmaster@dramatists.com www.dramatists.com

NEW PLAYS

★ **SHEL'S SHORTS by Shel Silverstein.** Lauded poet, songwriter and author of children's books, the incomparable Shel Silverstein's short plays are deeply infused with the same wicked sense of humor that made him famous. "...[a] childlike honesty and twisted sense of humor." *–Boston Herald.* "...terse dialogue and an absurdity laced with a tang of dread give [*Shel's Shorts*] more than a trace of Samuel Beckett's comic existentialism." *–Boston Phoenix.* [flexible casting] ISBN: 0-8222-1897-6

★ **AN ADULT EVENING OF SHEL SILVERSTEIN by Shel Silverstein.** Welcome to the darkly comic world of Shel Silverstein, a world where nothing is as it seems and where the most innocent conversation can turn menacing in an instant. These ten imaginative plays vary widely in content, but the style is unmistakable. "...[*An Adult Evening*] shows off Silverstein's virtuosic gift for wordplay...[and] sends the audience out...with a clear appreciation of human nature as perverse and laughable." *–NY Times.* [flexible casting] ISBN: 0-8222-1873-9

★ **WHERE'S MY MONEY? by John Patrick Shanley.** A caustic and sardonic vivisection of the institution of marriage, laced with the author's inimitable razor-sharp wit. "...Shanley's gift for acid-laced one-liners and emotionally tumescent exchanges is certainly potent..." *–Variety.* "...lively, smart, occasionally scary and rich in reverse wisdom." *–NY Times.* [3M, 3W] ISBN: 0-8222-1865-8

★ **A FEW STOUT INDIVIDUALS by John Guare.** A wonderfully screwy comedy-drama that figures Ulysses S. Grant in the throes of writing his memoirs, surrounded by a cast of fantastical characters, including the Emperor and Empress of Japan, the opera star Adelina Patti and Mark Twain. "Guare's smarts, passion and creativity skyrocket to awesome heights..." *–Star Ledger.* "...precisely the kind of good new play that you might call an everyday miracle...every minute of it is fresh and newly alive..." *–Village Voice.* [10M, 3W] ISBN: 0-8222-1907-7

★ **BREATH, BOOM by Kia Corthron.** A look at fourteen years in the life of Prix, a Bronx native, from her ruthless girl-gang leadership at sixteen through her coming to maturity at thirty. "...vivid world, believable and eye-opening, a place worthy of a dramatic visit, where no one would want to live but many have to." *–NY Times.* "...rich with humor, terse vernacular strength and gritty detail..." *–Variety.* [1M, 9W] ISBN: 0-8222-1849-6

★ **THE LATE HENRY MOSS by Sam Shepard.** Two antagonistic brothers, Ray and Earl, are brought together after their father, Henry Moss, is found dead in his seedy New Mexico home in this classic Shepard tale. "...His singular gift has been for building mysteries out of the ordinary ingredients of American family life..." *–NY Times.* "...rich moments ...Shepard finds gold." *–LA Times.* [7M, 1W] ISBN: 0-8222-1858-5

★ **THE CARPETBAGGER'S CHILDREN by Horton Foote.** One family's history spanning from the Civil War to WWII is recounted by three sisters in evocative, intertwining monologues. "...bittersweet music—[a] rhapsody of ambivalence...in its modest, garrulous way...theatrically daring." *–The New Yorker.* [3W] ISBN: 0-8222-1843-7

★ **THE NINA VARIATIONS by Steven Dietz.** In this funny, fierce and heartbreaking homage to *The Seagull*, Dietz puts Chekhov's star-crossed lovers in a room and doesn't let them out. "A perfect little jewel of a play..." *–Shepherdstown Chronicle.* "...a delightful revelation of a writer at play; and also an odd, haunting, moving theater piece of lingering beauty." *–Eastside Journal (Seattle).* [1M, 1W (flexible casting)] ISBN: 0-8222-1891-7

DRAMATISTS PLAY SERVICE, INC.
440 Park Avenue South, New York, NY 10016   212-683-8960   Fax 212-213-1539
postmaster@dramatists.com   www.dramatists.com